BACKPACKER®

Campsite
Cooking

COOKWARE, CUISINE, AND
CLEANING UP

Molly Absolon

Photographs by Dave Anderson

FALCONGUIDES

GUILFORD, CONNECTICUT
HELENA, MONTANA

AN IMPRINT OF GLOBE PEQUOT PRESS

To buy books in quantity for corporate use
or incentives, call **(800) 962–0973**
or e-mail **premiums@GlobePequot.com**.

FALCONGUIDES ®

Backpacker is a registered trademark of Cruz Bay Publishing, Inc.

FalconGuides is an imprint of Globe Pequot Press.

Falcon, FalconGuides, and Outfit Your Mind are registered trademarks of Morris Book Publishing, LLC.

Text design by Sheryl P. Kober
Page layout by Melissa Evarts

Library of Congress Cataloging-in-Publication Data
Absolon, Molly.
 Backpacker magazine's campsite cooking : cookware, cuisine, and cleaning up / Molly Absolon.
    p. cm. — (Falconguides)
 Includes bibliographical references and index.
 ISBN 978-0-7627-5650-6 (alk. paper)
 1. Outdoor cookery. I. Backpacker. II. Title. III. Title: Campsite cooking.
 TX823.A28 2010
 641.5'78—dc22

                                                                    2009046678

Printed in China

10 9 8 7 6 5 4 3 2 1

Contents

Chapter One:
Introduction to Campsite Cooking   1

Chapter Two:
Choosing a Kitchen Site   6

Chapter Three:
The Light and Fast Cook   10

Chapter Four:
Advanced Cooking   38

Chapter Five:
The Backcountry Gourmet   57

Chapter Six:
Lunch   65

Chapter Seven:
Washing Your Dishes   72

Chapter Eight:
Fires   77

Chapter Nine:
Water Purification   84

Chapter Ten:
Food Storage   86

Index   90

Nothing works up an appetite like living and working in the outdoors.

Chapter One
Introduction to Campsite Cooking

I pulled my sleeping bag up closer and snuggled in deeply. The scent of coffee wafted toward me from the kitchen, where Pete sat hunkered down by the stove. It was still dark. We were planning to climb Pingora, a classic rock spire in the Wind River Mountains and needed an early start. Pete brought me coffee in bed, along with a cup of steaming instant ramen noodles with a glop of cheese floating on the surface. It smelled delicious.

Food in the backcountry serves many functions: It gives you energy to accomplish your goals; it warms you up and gets you going when things are difficult; and it serves as a gathering point, a social focus for your expedition. You build up quite an appetite in the wilderness, and almost everything tastes good, including cheesy ramen soup at 4 a.m. I can't say I have ever eaten such a concoction in town, but out in the mountains, before a big climb, it hit the spot.

Preparing food in the wilderness can be as simple as heating water for ramen or as elaborate as baking bread. The complexity depends upon your desires, goals, and motivation, so before you head into the mountains, it behooves you to ask yourself—and your expedition mates—a few basic questions:

1. What's your goal for the trip?

2. Do you all like to cook or would you rather be climbing or fishing?

3. Does anyone have any special dietary needs?

4. How much can you carry?

GOALS

People go camping for all sorts of reasons. Some like to hike long miles, climb peaks, move camp often, and carry the minimum amount of gear. Others prefer to head to a destination and base camp, spending their days wandering nearby looking at birds, fishing, reading, and cooking. Some people travel with pack animals and bring everything from two-burner stoves, Dutch ovens, and coolers along with them, while others don't even bother to bring a stove. Where you fit in this spectrum is going to determine the type of food and equipment you will bring with you.

The critical thing is to make sure that everyone on your trip has some input into the food selection. All of us know that hungry people are cranky people, and the last thing you want is to spend your entire wilderness adventure listening to your tent mate

If your goal is to move quickly with a light pack, you'll probably opt for a basic menu.

whine about the food, especially if you were the one who came up with the menu. We also tend to make stupid decisions when we are hungry, so it's imperative that you have both enough food and food that is palatable to everyone to ensure you have a group of happy campers.

If you've been left with the task of planning the food for your trip, ask your teammates to fill out a questionnaire, expounding on their likes and dislikes. This will give you the information you need to come up with a plan that is acceptable for all.

WHAT KIND OF COOK ARE YOU?

Once you've identified your goals, you need to figure out what and how much food to bring. Planning a ration also includes determining the equipment you need and knowing how to prepare the food you bring along. Finally, you need to estimate the amount of fuel you will require. That's where this book comes in.

We've divided things up so you can start with the basics and build on your skills as you have the time and inclination. And remember: experiment. There's nothing like a bag full of powders, pasta, rice, beans, cheese, a spice kit, and all the time in the world to give you freedom to create.

It's fun to be creative cooking outdoors.

NOTE ON ORGANIZATION

This book has been divided into three basic categories: the light and fast cook, the advanced cook, and the backcountry gourmet. Within each category, we cover basic ration planning, offer hints on equipment, and provide a few sample recipes to get you going.

We also cover cooking techniques, fire building, and water purification to enable you to eat, drink, and be merry anywhere you go.

Chapter Two

Choosing a Kitchen Site

Have you ever noticed how most parties end up with everyone crowded into the kitchen? The same is true in the backcountry. The minute someone lights the stove and starts to prepare a meal, people begin to congregate for social hour, to have a hot drink, or to help out with the cooking. Because of this, you want to make sure you choose a good Leave No Trace location to site your kitchen.

Cooking on a rock slab leaves no impact, plus it's easy to keep your food out of the dirt.

LEAVE NO TRACE PRINCIPLES

The Leave No Trace program has established a set of basic principles designed to help guide people on ways to minimize their impact on wildlands. The goal of the program, which was started in 1994, is to allow people to enjoy the wilderness without loving it to death.

The seven principles are:

- » Plan ahead and prepare
- » Travel and camp on durable surfaces
- » Dispose of waste properly
- » Leave what you find
- » Minimize campfire impacts
- » Respect wildlife
- » Be considerate of other visitors

When it comes to siting your kitchen, the main principle that comes into play is camping on durable surfaces. We'll consider proper waste disposal and campfires later in this book.

What Is a Durable Surface?

Durable surfaces include rock, snow, established trails and campsites, gravel bars, beaches, and dry grasses. In popular camping areas, your best bet for a minimum-impact campsite is to use a preexisting one. That way you don't create new and unnecessary impacts. Stick within the confines of the site to avoid making it bigger; this means focusing your activities on places where the vegetation is already worn away and using existing trails to go to water or to your tents.

In a pristine area that has not seen a lot of use, you'll need to find naturally hardened sites for your camp kitchen. Look for large rock slabs or a gravely area, or try to find spots under trees where the vegetation is sparse or nonexistent. Avoid places where impacts from previous campers are just starting to be evident. Usually, if these places are left alone, they will recover.

Most public land managers require campsites to be 200 feet from water. This helps prevent water contamination and keeps you out of sight of other campers who may be spending the night in the vicinity. It also lessens the chance you'll disturb wildlife coming for water during the night. Carry a container to transport water so you don't have to go back and forth to fill up as you prepare your meal.

I like to separate my kitchen a bit from the tent areas. In bear country this separation is mandated and needs to be at least 200 feet. You don't need to go to that extreme if you aren't worried about bears; just a few feet will help reduce traffic in the tent area and cut down on impacts. Bring all your cook gear and food into the kitchen area so you don't have to

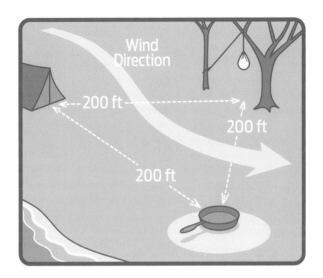

get up and move back and forth all the time looking for the butter or that extra pound of pasta you need to finish the meal.

Now you are ready to start cooking.

Chapter Three

The Light and Fast Cook

My 4 a.m. breakfast of ramen met all the criteria of a light and fast cook: It weighed very little, cooked up in a few minutes, and, with the lump of cheese floating around on top, was packed with calories to sustain me over the course of a long hard day of climbing. But cheesy ramen is not very creative, and your meals don't have to be that uninspiring. Light and fast does not always mean simply adding water and heat to some prepackaged concoction (although that works). You can get pretty creative—especially with some prep work at home—and still end up not having to carry much weight.

GO LIGHT

If you started backpacking in the sport's heyday—the 1970s—you have undoubtedly carried some pretty hefty packs in your time. Much of the early gear was army surplus, made from materials designed for durability rather than weight savings. I remember my first packs being so heavy I had to park them on a rock during rest breaks so I could get the load back on my back.

The simplicity of living, eating, and playing in the outdoors is part of camping's appeal.

The go-light backpacking movement first swept the country in the mid-'90s. A few enterprising outdoor enthusiasts realized that lighter packs made travel more enjoyable, and they began to improvise ways to shave ounces—even pounds—off their gear. The results have actually been quite profound. Lightweight backpackers can be a bit fanatical in their measures—cutting off labels and toothbrush handles and carrying nothing more than Pringles potato chips to eat—but the strategies they advocate and the gear they've influenced have filtered into mainstream

Today's camping gear is light, so backpacking is less painful than in the past.

Many freeze-dried meals can be rehydrated in their pouch, so you don't need to carry a bowl and there's no messy pot to clean up.

backpacking, and nowadays you rarely find people carrying the monster packs of yesteryear into the wilderness.

THE LIGHTWEIGHT KITCHEN

Before we get too far into the light and fast kitchen, we should say that you don't have to cook to eat well in the backcountry. You can carry food that requires no preparation—energy bars, cheese, packaged meats, crackers, bread, and so forth—and leave your kitchen behind. Your pack will be lighter, but that said, there's nothing like a hot meal to boost morale and energy after a hard day. So let's assume you plan at least to boil water on your trip.

My early backcountry kitchen included an Optimus 111B stove; two four-quart cooking pots with lids; a frying pan, also with a lid; a spatula; a mixing spoon; an eating spoon, a personal bowl, an insulated cup, and a water bottle per person; a multitool; pot grips; and a ladle, in addition to our food and fuel. If you are familiar with the 111B, you know these stoves were designed to be indestructible, and they were; they lasted for years and stood up to incredible abuse. They also weighed a ton because the heating

You can save weight by eating right out of the pot.

The Minimalist Kitchen (for a group of 2 to 4)

» **1–2 lightweight pots large enough to hold water to make drinks for the team (2–3 quarts)**
Consider titanium or aluminum to save weight.

» **Aluminum pie pan to serve as lid**
Pie pan can also act as someone's plate. Pack carefully to avoid puncturing.

» **Small channel-lock pliers**
Acts as pot grips and useful for repairs

» **Water bottle, heavy-duty plastic spoon, and titanium cup or bowl per person**
Water bottle can serve as a cup for hot drinks. Titanium cups are lightweight and can be used to heat water. If you are solo camping, leave the cup or bowl behind and eat out of your cook pot.

» **Serving spoon or spatula**
If someone in your group has a big metal spoon that can serve as a serving spoon, great. Otherwise, it's helpful to have one large spoon for mixing, serving, and so on. Also, it's more hygienic if you don't share your eating utensils. If you opt for a spatula, leave the spoon at home.

» **Water container**
You do not have to treat water used for cooking, but you want to avoid drinking untreated water accidentally. To avoid confusion, have a system in place. My system is: water in my personal bottle is always treated; water in the kitchen container never is.

If you pack a collapsible water container, you won't have to hike back and forth to your water source while cooking.

element came encased in a stainless steel box. My kitchen was overkill. Why I needed a ladle, a mixing spoon, an eating spoon, and a spatula is beside me. You don't have to have all that stuff, even if you are planning to cook an elaborate meal.

To really minimize your kitchen setup, choose items that can be used for a variety of purposes. A large titanium cup can also be used for cooking a meal for one person. Likewise, your eating spoon can serve as a mixing spoon and even a spatula for most purposes (okay, it doesn't do a very good job of flipping pancakes, but if pancakes aren't on the menu, you are probably fine). Use your water bottle for hot drinks, and leave the insulated mug at home. Bring a lightweight knife rather than a heavy multitool, unless the tool also serves as your all-purpose repair kit.

STOVES AND FUEL

Today you have a wide range of backpacking stoves available, ranging from homemade alcohol-burning contraptions that weigh as little as ten grams to expensive multifuel-burning stoves. Your choice will be dictated by several factors:

- » Price
- » Fuel availability
- » Menu demands
- » Number of people

If your goal is simply the lightest, cheapest option out there, build yourself an alcohol-burning stove out of aluminum cans (directions can be found on the Internet). The downside to this type of stove is that boiling water takes longer than it does with a blended-fuel cartridge or white-gas-burning stove, and you have less control over the heat output. But they are cheap and light, so it's worth experimenting with them to see if they will work for you.

Tests show that a top-mounted blended-fuel cartridge stove is the lightest, most efficient model in terms of its heat-to-weight ratio. These stoves do

Mixed-fuel stoves that can burn kerosene may be required if you plan to travel overseas, where fuels such as white gas are not available. Alcohol burns with the least intensity of all fuels, but the stoves are light and can be made at home. Fuel cartridges—most often containing a blend of butane and propane—are packed under pressure so they ignite easily without pumping or priming.

mixed fuel stove

alcohol stove

butane canister stove

Blended-fuel canister stoves are often the model of choice for climbers and mountaineers looking for a light, reliable stove.

not require priming, so they are simple to light. The downside is the fuel cartridges can be bulky and expensive, and they cannot be refilled. As a result, many of us end up with a box of half-full cartridges waiting to be used. Nonetheless, if your goal is to go light and fast, your best bet may be to opt for a top-mount blended-fuel cartridge or canister stove.

A top-mount cartridge stove will boil approximately thirty-three pints of water from a single eight-ounce canister. If you boil on average five pints of water per day, an eight-ounce canister will last you 6.7 days.

The MSR WhisperLite stove is a reliable backpacking stove.

White gas is usually cheaper than blended-fuel canisters, and you can refill your bottles before each trip. You do have to prime white gas, so lighting the stove is a little trickier than simply holding a flame to the fuel jet, but it just takes practice. For an all-around stove, you can't go wrong with a classic white-gas stove like the MSR WhisperLite. It's simple, easy to repair, and relatively light.

Typically, the WhisperLite will go through approximately one-third of a liter per day for a three-person group in the summer. You'll need more if you anticipate having to melt snow for water.

Finally, there are some other stove options available that are worth mentioning. For example, you can use a solid-fuel-burning stove. These stoves are tiny

Fill your white-gas fuel bottles away from the area where you will be cooking. Spilled fuel lights easily and can lead to an uncontrolled fire.

and light, and they burn solid-fuel tabs that fit in the palm of your hand. They are not incredibly hot, however, and fuel tabs are the most expensive fuel option out there, so these stoves aren't all that popular. But if you wish to be superlight, you may want to check one out.

The opposite extreme in terms of the cost of its fuel is a wood-burning stove. These stoves act as a chimney inside which you build a fire from small sticks and twigs to heat your food. Such stoves work well in places where wood is plentiful and dry. They become more persnickety when the weather turns foul.

Tips for Conserving Fuel

» Organize all your ingredients, fill your pots with water, and be ready to start cooking before you light your stove. No use wasting fuel warming the atmosphere because you forgot to fill the pot.

» Use a lid. A lid will keep the heat inside your pot and cause food to cook faster.

» Use a windscreen. The wind sucks heat away from your stove, and cooking takes a lot longer than it should. You can also conserve fuel by choosing a protected place for your kitchen.

» Don't let your pot bubble along merrily after it has reached a boil. The minute the water gets hot enough or your food is cooked, turn off the stove.

Prepping your ingredients and using a windscreen can help conserve fuel.

Finally, if you plan to travel outside the United States, you need to consider what fuel will be available. In many parts of the world, you cannot buy white gas or blended-fuel cartridges. For international travel, therefore, you may need a multifuel stove so you can burn whatever is available at your destination.

Stove Maintenance

Whatever type of stove you choose to carry, make sure you bring along—and know how to use—a simple repair kit. Stoves get clogged, brass fittings are stripped, and pumps may break, but most of these problems are easy to fix in the field if you have the right equipment.

With a simple repair kit, the WhisperLite stove is easy to fix in the field. Make sure you know how to clean and repair the stove you choose to carry.

MEAL PLANNING

Food often ends up being some of the bulkiest and heaviest items in your pack. You can minimize this weight by planning your meals carefully to ensure you have enough but not too much.

The simplest way to plan the food for a backpacking trip is to plan the menu for each meal. This method works well for shorter trips but can become cumbersome if your trip extends over a number of weeks. For longer trips you may find it's easier and more fun to buy food in bulk—pasta, rice, beans, sauces, cheese, and so on—and come up with a menu when you sit down to prepare each meal. We'll talk about bulk-ration planning in the next chapter; for the light and fast cook, let's stick to menu planning.

How you plan your meals is up to you, but one option is to divvy up the days amongst your team and have each team member plan meals for his or her designated days. So if there are four of you out for eight days, each of you will have two days' worth of meals for which you will be responsible. Make sure you talk to each other before you go to ensure you aren't all planning to cook the exact same thing.

What Kinds of Food?

If you really want the cooking to require a limited number of brain cells, you can buy dehydrated meals in a pouch and call it good. Today's dehydrated food

Freeze-dried food is the lightest option out there for backpackers, but it is also the most expensive.

has improved a lot over what used to be available, but it still tends to be relatively expensive per serving, and I think the meals all start to taste the same after a while. Furthermore, the serving sizes are notoriously small, so you probably want to double the amount recommended. That said, there's not much that can beat dehydrated meals for convenience: Boil water, and voilà, moments later you are enjoying a steaming bowl of Pasta Primavera or Beef Teriyaki.

If you want to avoid the cost but like the ease of dehydrated food, you can buy sauce packets in most supermarkets for a lot less money. Add a pound of pasta, and you and your tent mates can be eating pesto penne, spaghetti Alfredo, or any number of options with little more than some boiling water.

Coming Up with a Menu

Talk to your teammates about the types of foods they like to eat. Use a questionnaire. Then, with this information to guide you, map out the number of breakfasts, lunches, and dinners you'll need to plan for the duration of your trip. Let's say, for example, you'll be out for four nights with two friends (making your group a total of three). You'll need a total of four dinners, four breakfasts, and four lunches.

Sample Menu

Monday:
Breakfast and lunch:
On the road en route to trailhead

Dinner:
Macaroni and cheese (macaroni noodles, dried milk, sliced cheese—cheddar, Monterey Jack, your choice—garlic powder, salt and pepper)

Tuesday:
Breakfast:
Hot cereal (oatmeal, Cream of Wheat, and so on) with brown sugar, dried fruit, and nuts

Lunch (intended to be snacked on all day):
Summer sausage, cheese, crackers, bag of gorp, granola bars

Dinner:
Beans and rice (quick-cooking rice; dehydrated refried beans with such spices as salt, pepper, cumin, and red pepper flakes already added; cheddar cheese; hot sauce; dried veggies [optional])

Wednesday:
Breakfast:
Bagels with cheese or peanut butter

Lunch:
Tuna in vacuum-sealed packages, cheese, crackers, gorp, energy bar

Dinner:
Spaghetti (spaghetti noodles, tomato sauce, Parmesan cheese, dried veggies [optional])

Thursday:
Breakfast:
Rice pudding (rice, sugar, raisins, margarine, cinnamon, and nutmeg [mix up spices in small bag and pack with rice at home])

Lunch:
Sardines, crackers, cheese, cookies, dried fruit, candy

Dinner:
Pasta with spicy peanut sauce (penne or other type pasta; dried peanut sauce spiced with garlic, ginger, vinegar, red pepper flakes, sugar, soy sauce)

Hot cereal is warm, tasty, simple, and a great way to start the day. To add extra calories and fat for long days, add a spoonful of butter or peanut butter.

Friday:
Breakfast:
Hot cereal with brown sugar, dried fruit, and nuts

Lunch and dinner on the road home.

Miscellaneous:
Drinks:
Hot chocolate, coffee, tea, lemonade, Gatorade
(depending on your group preferences)
Condiments:
Margarine or butter, cooking oil, extra spices, hot sauce

Packaging Food

All the meals listed on this menu can be made in one pot. For organizational ease pack each meal together. You reduce your waste if you repackage food before you leave home. Pack everything into two-ply plastic bags. You can have your dried sauce mixes or beans in a separate plastic bag inside the larger bag of pasta or rice, so all you have to do when you sit down to cook is pull out the Monday dinner bag and you are on your way. This also precludes the need for a separate spice kit. Your meals come spiced if you've got the sauce already made at home or have mixed dried spices together in a special meal packet. You'll probably still want to bring salt and pepper and maybe some kind of hot sauce for people who like spicy food.

Boxes are bulkier and heavier than bags. They are also more difficult to pack.

How Much Do You Need?

A group of three can usually consume one pound of pasta plus sauce and cheese or a cup and a half of rice with half a pound of dried beans in a meal with ease in the backcountry. For steel-cut oats one cup will give you three cups of cooked oatmeal. You may want to round up portion sizes a bit if you have big eaters along, and remember, there's nothing like exercise and the great outdoors to cause your appetite to kick in.

When figuring amounts, consider these factors:

- » Group size
- » Duration of trip
- » Exertion level expected on trip
- » Weather
- » Altitude
- » Individual appetites (age of group weighs into this)
- » Food preferences
- » Weight of food

Most backpackers going out on a short summer trip need to consume approximately 2,500 to 3,000 calories a day. As your trip gets more challenging or the weather becomes colder, you will probably want closer to 3,500 calories per day. If you are going to be out in the winter, you should allocate as much as 4,000 to 5,000 calories per person per day! That's a lot of food, but it takes a lot of calories to keep your engine going when the temperatures are below freezing and you are working hard. Compare these amounts to a typical office worker or homemaker who needs between 1,400 and 2,500 calories per day.

Nutritional Concerns

For a short trip you don't have to spend a lot of time worrying about how your menu compares with the U.S. Recommended Daily Nutritional Allowances. Use your judgment, and include variety in your food, and you should be fine. Just keep a few basics in mind:

Carbohydrates: Provide quick energy and should make up at least 50 percent of your daily caloric intake. Examples of carbs are breads, cereal, pasta, rice, and dehydrated fruits.

Fats: Fat contains more than twice as many calories per pound as carbohydrates and are the body's major source of stored energy. Generally speaking, fats should provide about one-fifth of your daily intake of calories, but on hard wilderness trips this proportion should be higher. Fats aren't converted to energy as quickly as carbs, so they allow us to go without eating for long periods of time and are therefore a great source of energy on long, hard days. Fats are found in cheese, butter, nuts, peanut butter, cooking oil, and margarine.

Proteins: Proteins serve a number of different functions in our bodies. They act as enzymes, antibodies, hormones, and building materials. They play a role in blood clotting; transporting fats, minerals, and oxygen; and helping us balance our fluid and electrolyte levels. So it's pretty important to have enough protein in your diet. You get complete proteins from animal foods—meat, poultry, fish, eggs, milk, and cheese—and soybeans. Plant foods contain partial proteins, so they need to be combined to make a complete protein (examples of combos that result in a complete protein include rice and beans, bread and peanut butter, and hot cereal with reconstituted dry milk). You can also buy protein bars to provide you with complete proteins.

Special Treats

Okay, you want to have a balanced diet when you are camping, but being outdoors and exercising from dawn to dusk is also a time to relax a little. Treats can add some enjoyment to your trip, especially at the end of a long, hard, hot day of hiking or when it's been raining nonstop for hours. I like to have each person I'm camping with bring something a little special to pull out when the going gets rough. It may be a candy bar for everyone or some hard candy. It may be a dessert such as instant cheesecake or a bag of homemade cookies. Some people opt for savory snacks such as vacuum-sealed smoked salmon. You don't have to be extravagant in your extras, but the element of surprise and a little bit of novelty can brighten up your day in a matter of seconds.

COOKING TECHNIQUES

For the light and fast cook, the main thing you need to know how to do is boil water. One-pot meals are pretty self-explanatory: bring your water to a boil, add pasta (or with rice add rice and water and then bring to a boil), simmer until soft, drain.

To reconstitute your sauces, pour the excess pasta water into someone's cup and mix the sauce up before adding it to the cooked pasta.

Cooking Tricks to Avoid Catastrophe

» With pasta always make sure you have plenty of water, at least three parts water to one part pasta. This keeps you from ending up with one big, partially cooked, stuck-together pasta blob.

» To drain your pasta, place a lid over the pot and with wool gloves on your hands to protect them from the heat, tilt the pot just enough to let the water flow. Remember, the pasta is likely to fall onto the lid in a sudden plop, so be ready for that to avoid dumping your dinner onto the ground.

» If your stove is cooking too quickly, depressurize it, and the roaring flame will dim to a flicker. On a white gas stove, the best way to depressurize is to turn the stove off, blow out the flame, unscrew the fuel pump, and let some pressure escape, then rescrew the pump and relight the stove.

» If you smell burning, don't stir! Remove the pot from the heat immediately. Stirring spreads the burn taste. If your food needs more cooking, transfer the uncooked portions into people's bowls; clean the pot and resume cooking. Make sure your pots are clean before you cook. Food sticks more readily to dirty surfaces.

» Don't overspice! People have a wide range of taste preferences from bland to scorching hot; your best bet is to be gentle with your spices, then let people add if necessary.

» If conditions are cold and wet and people need extra calories, add a lump of margarine, butter, cheese, or peanut butter to your meal. The extra dose of fat will help restore depleted calories.

» You do not have to use disinfected water when cooking. If the water simmers or the bread bakes, you've killed off any dangerous germs.

» One of the main reasons people get sick in the backcountry is not untreated water—those bugs usually get you after you return home—it's fecal contamination and shared germs. Yuck. Don't share the nasties. Wash your hands thoroughly before you begin cooking, and don't use your personal spoon for a taste test. Put a sample of whatever you are cooking in your bowl and take a bite. You'll all be happier if you stay healthy.

Cooking is more enjoyable if you are organized. Keep your ingredients handy, and divvy up tasks to make life easier when you get into camp.

STAYING ORGANIZED

An organized kitchen makes cooking enjoyable whether you are in the woods or back at home. I typically fall into a pattern when I get to camp at the end of the day. First, someone goes and fills up the water bladder. Then if the temperatures are cool or the weather wet, I'll usually pull out the stove and start water for hot drinks while people set up their tents. This helps tide people over until dinner is ready.

Once camp is set and you've changed out of your hiking boots, look for a comfortable, low-impact spot to site your kitchen. Pull out all the ingredients you will need for the meal, including hot drinks and spices,

Macaroni and Cheese

(serves 3)

For me no backpacking trip is complete without at least one meal of mac and cheese. Fast, filling, and yummy, mac and cheese is comfort food wherever you are!

1 lb. pasta

1 cup or more diced cheese (cheddar is the classic cheese for mac and cheese, but you can experiment with other cheese flavors for variety. Avoid too much mozzarella, as it makes your sauce very stringy.)

3–4 Tbsp butter or margarine

4 Tbsp dried milk (add enough water to make it look like milk!)

Salt, pepper, garlic powder to taste

Boil water, and add pasta. Boil until done; the time depends on the pasta type, but it usually takes between eight and twelve minutes. Stir occasionally to keep the pasta from sticking. Remove from heat. Drain water, leaving an inch or so in the bottom of the pot; add milk mixture and spices, and stir to coat pasta. Add cheese and margarine, and stir. Return pot to stove, and heat slowly, stirring constantly until cheese melts. Add salt and pepper to taste.

Alternatives: Sometimes it's fun to bring some special spices to liven up your food. Add some red pepper flakes to put some zing into your mac and cheese, or for a more subtle Italian-style flavoring, use such spices as oregano, rosemary, or basil. If you've brought along a frying pan, fry the whole concoction up for delicious fried macs. Finally, to make your macs creamier, add more milk.

and gather your pots, water, and utensils so they are within easy reach. Make sure your stove is full (but don't fill up fuel bottles in the kitchen—spilled gas can ignite and cause a fire if you aren't careful). Now you are ready to go.

SAFETY IN THE KITCHEN

Whenever you start combining fire and gas, you introduce danger. Not only do you risk setting the forest on fire if you mishandle your stove and fuel, it's also easy to get burned. Make sure you set your kitchen up in an area where there's not much to catch fire, such as on a rock or in a campsite where there is no vegetation. Keep a supply of water on hand to douse any flames that escape.

Be careful around pots full of boiling water. Make sure your stove is stable so the pot cannot fall off and dump boiling water in your lap. Keep your face averted from the stove when you light it to avoid singeing your eyebrows and hair if the stove flares up. Make sure you use either pot grips or thick wool gloves to move hot pans.

If you do end up burning yourself, immediately douse the area with cold water. Keep running cold water over the burn for 20 minutes or more (depending on the size of the injury). Once you've removed the heat from the site, use your first-aid training to treat the wound.

Chapter Four
Advanced Cooking

If the goal for your trip is a bit more food oriented, or you plan to be out long enough that you think one-pot glop could get old, it doesn't take much effort to step up a bit and move into advanced outdoor cooking. The main difference really is that you bring along a frying pan and you start baking quick breads, making casseroles or layered dishes, and frying things like hash brown potatoes and freshly caught trout. I love having a frying pan because of the variety it adds to the menu, in terms of both substance and texture. Too many days in the mountains eating food that has no crunch begins to get to me after a while. You may not be adding the texture of fresh produce, but you do get the substance of bread and the crispy flavor of fried cheese when you use a frying pan.

Another thing many advanced cooks do to add variety to their outdoor cooking is to ditch the meal plan and pack bulk food instead. This technique involves bringing a balance of different food types—pasta, rice, sauces, flour, beans, and, most importantly, a spice kit—that you can mix and match to create any number of meal options. So on a cold, rainy night when everyone wants instant gratification, you may choose to whip up a quick pot of mac and cheese. But when you have a rest day and the sun is

Wow your friends with piping hot pizza. It's easy, tasty, and a nice change from one-pot glop.

out, you have the option of making something more elaborate: corn bread with cheesy beans or fresh-baked pizza.

Bulk rationing is not for everyone. Ideally suited for long trips with big groups, this method can save money as well as add an element of creativity to your diet, but some people still prefer to stick to menu planning because of its inherent simplicity. Cooking with the bulk method always requires more effort and thought; some people find this inspiring, while others are intimidated by a bagful of ingredients with no directions. You decide. It's worth experimenting to see what method you prefer.

THE ADVANCED KITCHEN

You really don't need that much more equipment to advance your cooking techniques. As mentioned above, the key addition is a frying pan. Finding a good frying pan can be tricky. You want a lightweight option, and you also want a flat lid that you can build a fire on (more on that later), finally you don't want the pan or lid to have any plastic parts. On many frying pans you can simply remove plastic handles and knobs to transform it into a backcountry utensil. I'm a big fan of the Banks Fry/Bake pan. The National Outdoor Leadership School has been using these pans since 1979, and the reason is that they work. They are relatively lightweight (although no dyed-in-the-wool light-and-fast backpacker would be caught carrying one), and the lids are designed to hold a fire. They are pricey, but with a little care, they will last you for years.

Otherwise the only real addition you need to your cook gear is a pair of 100 percent wool gloves. Wool gloves make baking much easier. They serve as potholders, allowing you to rotate your pan, thereby ensuring the heat is distributed evenly. They are also great for staying warm on a cold day.

Extras for Advanced Cooking

» Frying pan   » Wool gloves   » Spatula   » Spice kit

The addition of a frying pan and spatula brings versatility to your meal options.

BULK-RATION PLANNING

With a bulk-ration, you head out on your camping trip without any real plan for what you'll eat, when, and how. On the surface this sounds risky, and there is a chance that on your last night out you may end up with an odd assortment of ingredients to make a dinner from, but who knows, that creative combination may turn out to be your best meal for the entire trip.

Outdoor professionals often use bulk rationing because it is less expensive than buying prepared foods, and because it gives participants room to experiment. The systems that have been developed over the years are designed to provide enough guidelines to ensure you have balance in your ingredients.

Preplanning Considerations

Your first step in determining how much food you need for your trip requires that you consider the same factors you considered when planning a more rigid menu. You need to know your group size and age, trip length, exertion level, potential weather, altitude, and individual food preferences. Other concerns are perishability and diet restrictions. Once you've answered these questions, you can begin to get a sense of how much food you can expect to consume on a daily basis.

This amount will vary. On a short summer backpacking trip, you can usually get by on one and a half pounds per person per day. As the weather worsens or the difficulty of the trip increases, this amount will have to increase.

Guidelines for Food Amounts		
1.5 lbs per person per day	· Warm days and nights · Group includes children, older adults · Low-intensity activities · High altitude	· 2,500–3,000 calories per person per day
1.75–2 lbs per person per day	· Warm days, cool nights · Hiking with full packs for > 7 days or more intense activity · Younger participants	· 3,000–3,500 calories per person per day
2–2.5 lbs per person per day	· Cool days and nights, chance of rain or snow · High level of physical activity (hiking, climbing, skiing, and so on)	· 3,500–4,000 calories per person per day
> 2.5 lbs per person per day	· Cold days and cold nights (e.g., winter camping) · Strenuous activity (mountaineering, skiing)	· 4,000–5,000 calories per person per day

These guidelines are based on the figures developed at the National Outdoor Leadership School after years of experimentation.

Once you have calculated the amount of food per person you expect you'll need, multiply that number by the number of participants and the number of days for the total poundage you will need.

For example, you are traveling with your wife and two teenage children on a four-day summer backpacking trip. Teenagers can be big eaters, but the trip's goals are modest, so you are probably safe planning on one and a half pounds per person. That means your calculation is 4 days x 4 people x 1.5 lbs per person = 24 lbs total.

So you need twenty-four pounds, but twenty-four pounds of what? Your next step is to divide this

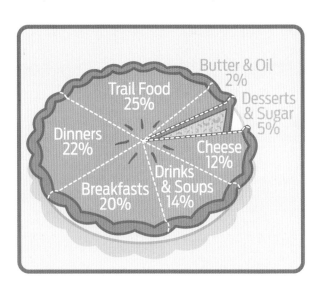

number into various categories to ensure you have adequate variety and balance.

For your four-day trip, figure the amount of dinner food you'll need as follows: 24 pounds x .22 = 5.28 or approximately 5¼ pounds of dinner foods.

Typically, dinner foods will be pasta, beans, rice, couscous, and other staples. Breakfast foods include freeze-dried shredded potatoes, hot cereals, pancake mix, and granola. You can buy all these items in a grocery store, or better yet, buy the staples in the bulk section of a natural foods store.

Repackaging Food

Before you head into the mountains, take time to repackage your food in heavyweight plastic bags. It helps to bag your food in uniform weights, just so you have a sense of how much is in each bag. One-pound increments is a good standard: The bags aren't too bulky to pack, and one pound of pasta or rice is usually a good base amount for most meals.

Spices can be packed in small plastic bags or Nalgene bottles with screw-top caps. The bottle option is heavier, but they are pretty convenient when you are cooking. Liquid spices—oil, soy sauce, vinegar, and so on—are best packed in Nalgene because the bottles are less likely to be punctured than thin-walled plastic. You may want to pack your oil bottle in a plastic bag so it won't make a mess if you spring a leak. Likewise, it is a good idea

A few spices can liven up even the simplest meal.

Spice Kits

Spice kits can be as elaborate or bare bones as you like. Here are just some ideas for spices that are can help add variety to your meals.

Salt and pepper

Garlic powder: flavoring for soups, main dishes, sauces

Cumin: flavoring for beans, rice, potatoes; good for both Indian- and Mexican-inspired dishes

Italian seasonings (or basil and oregano): flavoring for tomato sauce, pasta dishes, potatoes

Curry: flavoring for Asian dishes, rice, and so on

Cinnamon: good for sweet breads, hot cereal, and hot drinks

Baking powder: leavening agent for quick breads

Dill: good for soups, potatoes, fish, breads

Cayenne: good for a little heat with beans, curries, and other spicy dishes

Oil: for sautéing or frying

Soy sauce: flavoring for Asian-inspired dishes or as an all-around additive to rice, pasta, popcorn

Vanilla: adds flavor to sweet breads, hot drinks, hot cereal

Vinegar: adds tang to sauces

Hot sauce: great condiment for adding (or covering up) flavor and heat in main dishes

to double-bag your margarine or butter to prevent leakage in your pack.

When you load up your food, pack breakable items such as crackers or tortillas in pots or frying pans to prolong their shape. You also want to make sure that you pack your food above your fuel, just in case. Spilled fuel will destroy your food and cut short your trip.

COOKING TIPS

As mentioned before, a frying pan is the door to your new world of outdoor cooking. With a frying pan and a lid, you can create crispy hash browns and breaded pan-fried trout; you can sauté spices and brown nuts for curries; or if you are more ambitious, you can bake pizza, cinnamon rolls, calzones, or coffee cake.

Frying

Frying doesn't require much skill, but there are a few rules of thumb to ensure your success:

» Don't be afraid to use a lot of oil or butter. (Remember, you're burning lots of calories out there! If you skimp on the oil, you aren't going to get nice crispy hash browns or toasted bagels.)
» Don't stir. (If you stir too much, you'll never get your food to brown, and you may end up with

mush. Let your food sizzle, and then flip it over without stirring. You'll be much happier with the results.)

» Don't be afraid to burn. (Obviously, it is not your goal to burn your food, but you want to give it time to cook to obtain a nice crispy crust. So let the food sit for a while, longer than you may think, before flipping it over to brown the other side.)

Baking

The easiest form of baking is the flip method. The name says it all: You bake your dough on one side, then flip it over to bake the other. The flip method works best for stiff dough—biscuits, flat breads, calzones—things that hold their shape.

To flip-bake, grease your frying pan, place your bread in the center of the pan, and cover. Lower the stove to its lowest possible setting. You may need to depressurize white gas stoves to get a low-enough flame. I like to make a platform with my aluminum windscreen and place the frying pan on the platform so it is somewhat removed from the heat.

You can also take a rock that is the height of your stove and set one side of the frying pan on the rock, the other over the flame.

With this method you'll want to rotate the pan "around the clock" to ensure that all sides are cooked evenly. Set a small rock on the frying pan lid to indicate

One way to slow down your cooking time for baking is to distance the pan from the flame by balancing it on top of your windscreen.

Balance your pan between a rock and your stove to make sure things bake evenly.

your starting point; let's call it 12 o'clock. After four or five minutes at twelve, rotate the pan so that 3 o'clock is over the heat, and wait another four or five minutes. Repeat the process for 6 o'clock and 9.

Once you've gone around the clock once, remove your pan from the heat and uncover. Gently lift a

Think of your pan as a clock and rotate through the hours systematically.

corner of your bread to see if it is stiff and brown. If so, you are ready to flip. If not, give it a few more minutes. To flip effectively, take a spatula and slide it under the bread. Make sure it is completely detached from the pan. Once the bread is totally free, flip it. For larger bread products you can slide the bread onto a pot lid, and then flip the pot lid over so the bread falls into the frying pan with the uncooked side down.

For stiff breads, flip baking is a simple way to cook both the top and bottom evenly.

Pizza

Yeast breads sound intimidating, but they can be pretty straightforward and are a great way to impress your tent mates. Use this basic dough recipe for pizza, as well as for calzones and bread.

1 Tbsp yeast
1 part warm water
3 parts flour (mixture of white and whole wheat works well. For lighter breads, use more white. For denser, chewier breads, go heavy on the whole wheat.)
½ tsp salt

For one pizza use one cup water to three cups flour. To make more dough, increase the amount while maintaining the three-to-one-to-one ratio (flour-water-yeast).

Mix warm water with yeast, and let sit for five minutes. Mixture should get frothy. Add one-third of your flour and salt to the yeast mixture, and stir thoroughly. Mix remaining flour into yeast mixture slowly, stirring well after each addition. Once the dough is relatively dry and mixed, begin kneading (make sure your hands are clean!). You can knead right in the pot without any problem. Flour your hands to help keep the dough from sticking, and add more flour if the dough is too wet. Knead for five or ten minutes. The dough should feel smooth and elastic. Brush the dough lightly with oil, and place in a warm spot to rise. You can put the dough in a plastic bag to rise, or if it's cold out, you can even wear your dough under your shirt to keep it warm while rising.

Meanwhile, make your tomato sauce.

Tomato Sauce:
2 Tbsp dried veggies (combination of onions and peppers works well)
1 cup water
¼–½ cup powdered tomato base
Spices: garlic, oregano, basil, salt and pepper to taste

Rehydrate dried vegetables in hot water for ten minutes. Stir in remaining ingredients and heat, stirring occasionally. You can vary your thickness by adding or subtracting water.

Putting it all together:
Let dough rise for about one hour or until it has doubled in size. Press two fingers into the dough; if an indentation remains, the dough is ready. Punch down dough, and shape into pizza form. Bake over low heat using the round-the-clock method until bottom is cooked. Flip dough, cover with tomato sauce and cheese, and bake slowly until cheese is melted. (You can place a few drops of water into the fry pan and cover quickly to make steam and speed up the cheese melting.)

Calzone variation: For calzones, follow basic dough recipe to the final shaping steps. Punch dough out into pizza form, then cover half of the top surface with tomato sauce and cheese. Fold the uncovered side over on top of the sauce, and pinch closed along the edge. Bake until dough is firm, flip, and bake other side.

Use this basic dough recipe for other things like cinnamon rolls. To make cinnamon rolls, spread butter, sugar, cinnamon, and raisins evenly across the top of your dough instead of tomato sauce. Roll the mixture up into a log, and slice into 1½-inch-thick discs. Bake as normal.

Casseroles

Layering sauces, noodles, and cheese in the frying pan and baking into a yummy casserole is a great way to add some variety and texture to your meals. Basically, you'll be modeling your meal after a classic lasagna dish, alternating cheese, sauce, noodles, cheese, sauce, noodles. But don't limit yourself to tomato sauce and noodles. You can make casseroles out of just about anything. For example, make a tortilla pie by alternating cheese, tortillas, and refried beans. Or make scalloped potatoes with freeze-dried potato slices layered with cheese and a creamy white sauce.

Here are a few helpful tips for creating a successful casserole: First, start with cheese on the bottom of your pan so you end up with a nice crispy bottom layer. Second, make sure there is enough liquid in your sauce to keep things moist and bubbly. At the same time, you don't want so much water in the pan that

---

Lasagna Hint

You can make a kind of pseudo ricotta cheese for your lasagna by mixing up dried milk with water and a teaspoon or so of vinegar. Mix the milk to a gruel-like consistency, then add the vinegar. Pour the mixture in between a layer of noodles and cheese.

---

everything is floating around. Think of your casserole as a solid, not a liquid. You can always add a bit of water at the end to create some steam for melting the cheese on top. Finally, make sure your uppermost layer is cheese or sauce to keep noodles or tortillas from drying out.

Casseroles work best if the ingredients are pre-cooked. So cook your noodles or rehydrate your potatoes and beans before combining everything in the frying pan. Then when you bake the final concoction, you'll only need to heat it enough to make sure it is warm and the cheese is melted, rather than having to cook everything through. Use the same round-the-clock baking technique we've already discussed to ensure even heating.

Chapter Five

The Backcountry Gourmet

Don't be intimidated by the title; any of us can be a backcountry gourmet if we're willing to experiment with our ingredients. For the purposes of this book, the main difference between the advanced cook and the backcountry gourmet is that now we'll be adding a top source of heat when baking to create more of an oven effect. Applying heat both above and below allows you to cook your food slowly and evenly, thus enabling you to bake cakes or work with batters of moister consistency that cannot be flipped readily.

GOURMET BAKING

It doesn't take much to impress your tent mates. Think how happy they'll be if you whip up a chocolate birthday cake miles from the nearest oven. The truth is, baking a cake can be pretty simple. The key is providing a steady source of low heat from both below and above your pan. Some people carry along an aluminum "pot parka." Basically, a pot parka is a kind of tent made from nonflammable material that you can lower over your frying pan to create an ovenlike space for holding in heat.

If you do not have a pot parka, the other tried-and-true method for creating heat above your frying

The Outback Oven is a commercial pot parka that creates a convection dome over your backpacking stove to make baking easy.

For twiggy fires, your sticks should be no thicker than your thumb.

pan is to build a fire on top of the lid to create an oven. Start by gathering up a pile of small (finger-sized) twigs. Then grease and flour your frying pan, pour in your batter, and cover the pan with a lid. Don't over-fill the pan. If your batter touches the top, it will burn. Give yourself at least an inch of clearance so the batter can rise without reaching the top or overflowing.

Set up the stove as you do for the flip method— either with a rock to counterbalance your pan or with the windscreen set up as an elevated platform—but before you put your frying pan on the stove, place three thumb-sized twigs over the flames until they catch fire. Once the twigs are burning cheerfully, transfer them to the lid of your frying pan and add more twigs to get a small fire going. Now place the frying pan on the stove, and begin your baking. If you happen to have a campfire going, rather than building a twiggy fire simply scoop up some coals from the fire with a pot lid or shovel, place the coals on the frying

Different Batter and Dough Consistencies

» If you can pour the batter, it's best for pancakes or cake batter.

» If your batter is thicker and falls off your spoon in glops, it's perfect for biscuits.

» If your dough is thick and dry enough to form a ball that you can handle without getting your fingers covered with tacky dough, then it's perfect for bread.

» You can mix and match white and wheat flour in most recipes. The more wheat flour you use, the denser and heavier the bread. White flour makes lighter, fluffier breads.

pan lid, and let them serve as the source of top heat.

This baking method is not for children, as you are definitely playing with fire. Twiggy fires need constant attention, not only to ensure burning sticks don't roll off the lid and start a larger blaze but also because the small sticks burn out quickly so you need to constantly feed the flame. Be patient. Let your pan complete its clock rotation—which should take about 20 minutes—before you check to see if your bread is cooked. When the time comes to check, remove the frying pan lid carefully—remember you are moving a fire. Use your pot grips and plan out your route before you start. Make sure no one is in the way and that you aren't carrying coals or burning sticks over something flammable such as your nylon clothing or a bunch of dry grass. I like to place the lid on a large rock where there is nothing to catch fire if a coal happens to

You can light your twigs by holding them in the stove flame.

Bean and Corn Bread Pie

Corn bread:
1 cup cornmeal
¾ cup flour
½ cup powdered milk
1 Tbsp baking powder
1 tsp salt
1½ cup cold water
3 Tbsp honey or brown sugar

Beans:
½ lb instant dried beans (refried or black beans work well)
1 cup hot water
Dried onions or peppers if you have them
½ tsp cumin
Red pepper flakes (to taste)
Salt and pepper (to taste)

1 cup sliced cheese (cheddar, Monterey Jack, pepper jack)

Mix all ingredients to make corn bread batter; set aside. Mix up bean mixture. Grease and flour your frying pan. Pour one-half of the corn bread mixture into the frying pan. Cover corn bread with all of the bean mixture, spread evenly across the pan. Cover beans with sliced cheese. Pour remaining corn bread batter over the cheese. Cover and bake for 20 to 30 minutes.

You can create your own backpacking oven by building a small fire on top of your frying pan lid.

escape. If the food is cooked, I'll just leave the twiggy fire to burn itself out in the safe place.

If you have made a cake or corn bread, you can tell if your meal is done by inserting a knife into the center of the batter. If the bread is cooked through, the knife will come out clean. For yeast breads, check to see if they are cooked by thumping them with your finger; the bread is done if it sounds hollow.

Chapter Six

Lunch

For most backpackers lunch starts the minute break-fast is over and ends when dinner begins. That's because like any endurance activity, you need to maintain a constant supply of calories to keep yourself from bonking. So most of us tend to snack all day on the trail.

GOOD SNACKING

Lunch foods are one of the areas you may struggle with because of different preferences in your group. Some people may love garlic-flavored snack mix, while others hate it yet love cheese-covered sesame sticks. It helps, therefore, to pack a wide variety of snacks.

Your primary goals are:

> » Palatability
> » Packability
> » Perishability
> » Variety

Snack Mixes

Most bulk-food sections of natural food stores have bins filled with all sorts of different snack mixes. There are cracker mixes, fruit mixes, spicy mixes, sweet mixes, mixes with chocolate, and mixes with pretzels.

Pouring snack foods into your hands rather than digging through the bag helps minimize the spread of germs.

It's nice to have a selection to choose from when you are out in the mountains, so buy a few pounds of different options.

Mix It Up!

You can make your own trail mix. Gorp (good old-fashioned raisins and peanuts) is an easy favorite, especially if you add chocolate chips or M&M's to the mix.

Add some fun to your homemade mixes by experimenting with ingredients. Use dried cherries, cranraisins, or strawberries instead of the normal raisin option. Try tamari-covered almonds or rice crackers. You can find lots of nuts and fruits to try in your trail mix in the bulk-food section.

Making your own mix can be cheaper but not always, so if cost is a concern, it is worth taking a moment to calculate whether you'll spend more buying a pound of a premade mix or you'll save by buying peanuts, raisins, or whatever else separately and mixing up your own concoction.

Dried Fruit

Dried fruit provides concentrated calories and a naturally sweet alternative to candy for snacking along the trail. You can also chop up dried fruit to use in sweet breads and hot cereals. Be careful not to eat too much dried fruit in one sitting, however, as the fruit does reasbsorb water in your system and can leave you feeling bloated or with a stomachache if you overindulge. If you're feeling adventurous, try drying your own fruit at home either in a dehydrator or in the sun. Bananas, mangos, apricots, apples, grapes, and papaya can all be dried (or purchased dried) and make a great trailside snack.

Crackers and Breads

It's nice to have something to accompany cheese and meats on the trail, and bread and crackers are the logical option. Look for hard breads that can withstand the rigors of being stuffed into a backpack: Bagels or pita bread work well. Crackers need to be packed carefully to ensure you end up with something besides a bag of crumbs. Neither crackers nor bread lasts very long in the backcountry, so plan on using these items up during the first couple of days of your trip.

Cheese and Meat

Cheese, summer sausage or salami, tuna in vacuum-sealed packages, smoked salmon, and sardines all make great trail food and are a good source of

Mix and match your lunchtime snacks for variety and nutritional balance.

protein. The trick with these items is that once you break the seal on their packaging they tend to spoil quickly. So you should plan on consuming most of the item in one sitting.

Energy Bars, Gels, and So On

There are countless energy foods on the market, from shots of glucose-rich syrups to gummy-bear-like cubes. You can buy "real food" bars or space-age energy bars that bear little resemblance to any food you have ever placed on your table. Energy foods are a great concentrated source of calories and some-times nutrients and protein (read the label!). They can be a good pick-me-up on a long, hard day or can serve as a meal replacement in a pinch. They do tend to be rather expensive, so I usually carry them to supplement my lunch food rather than having them serve as one of the mainstays.

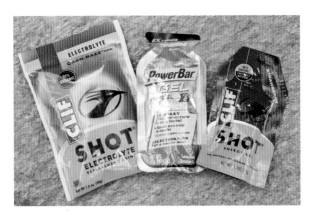

You have many choices in energy bars, shots, and gels these days. Make sure you like the flavor of your choice. People seem to have strong preferences when it comes to different energy foods.

Candy, Cookies, and Other Sweets

It's nice to have some sweet treats on long trips, so I tend to bring along some candy bars, cookies or hard candy. Don't forego more nutritious options for these treats; remember, they are there for special occasions but should not replace food that is better for you.

PACKING YOUR LUNCHES

Lunch food can be a bit challenging to share if you hike at different paces from your partners or if you happen to be heading out in different directions for the day. You can also run into trouble if Suzy Q always seems to end up with your favorite trail mix or Little Johnny makes a habit of mining through the bag to find every last bit of chocolate. So sometimes it helps to discuss this issue to make sure there are no hard feelings about who is eating what. You may opt to make individual bags of gorp so people can eat mindlessly without worrying too much about eating more than their share. The main point is to make sure you all have talked about how to share the lunch food equitably before you hit the trail.

Chapter Seven

Washing Your Dishes

The best way to make cleanup easy is to eat everything in your pot. That's where accuracy in your menu planning helps. The most experienced outdoorspeople know how to pack enough, but not too much, food to keep everyone happy and healthy for the duration of their trip. That said, you are going to have to clean your pots at some point, so here's a few tips to guide you.

DISPOSE OF WASTE PROPERLY

Leftovers, food scraps, even washing water need to be disposed of properly to avoid attracting animals to your campsite. Your motivation here is twofold: Number one, you don't want to wake up to a bear—or even a less dangerous but annoying mouse—pawing around your kitchen. Number two: Animals that become habituated to humans often end up dying. Either they are killed because they are dangerous—as in the case of many bears—or they become sick or malnourished. So either way you look at it, your best bet is to make sure you are not inadvertently feeding wildlife with your kitchen scraps.

Strain your wash water to remove leftovers. Bag and carry out these scraps with your other garbage.

Once your dishwater is free of floaties, you have a choice. In most parts of the country, the best practice is to fling the water around you so it is scattered over a wide area. The only time this technique is not recommended is in grizzly bear country or heavily used areas like desert river corridors. With bears you want to concentrate and minimize odors, so your best option is to dig a cathole (a hole approximately 6 inches deep) and pour the wastewater in. If you are camped by a large, silty river, such as the Colorado, you may opt to pour your gray water directly into the main flow of the river.

Check with the land management agency that is responsible for the area you are camping in to find out what method they recommend for disposing of wash water.

Scrape visible food scraps into a plastic bag, and pack them out with your trash.

To broadcast means to toss the water widely, dispersing it over as large an area as possible.

TRICKS FOR GETTING THE POTS CLEAN

Some people like to bring along biodegradable soap for cleaning their dishes; others do not. I happen to fall in the second camp. If you do bring soap, make sure you've rinsed the pot clean to remove any soapy residue. Soapy pots can give your food an unwanted flavor or, worse, make you sick.

I find the best technique is to heat up a quarter of a pot of water to help soften the cooked-on residue from your meal. You can then use your fingers to pick and scrape away at the food. This usually works on all but the most stubborn burnt-on gunk (one good reason not to burn your food!). You can also use a metal spoon or spatula to scrape away at the pot. To ensure that your pots are germ free, rinse with boiling water and dry in the sun or with a clean cloth.

In some situations, it helps to use a handful of dirt or sand to scrub at your dishes. The problem with this technique is that then you end up with sand impregnated with fatty food residue—it's hard to dispose of that without leaving a smelly mound of dirt behind. Some people like to bring a scrubby or sponge along to help clean pots, but if you are out more than a few days, most sponges or scrubbies tend to turn into festering, germ-laden blobs pretty quickly. You can boil them, but that seems like a waste of fuel and time when I've found fingers and warm water really work the best.

WHERE DO YOU WASH YOUR DISHES?

You don't want to contaminate your water sources, so always wash your dishes 200 feet from streams, lakes, and rivers unless the local bear camping regulations say otherwise (in some parts of Alaska, for instance, regulations call for you to wash your dishes in the rivers).

PERSONAL HYGIENE

Camping is about getting dirty and maybe a little smellier than normal, but it's not about being unhygienic. Dirty hands spread disease in the backcountry as much as they do in town, so just as at home, always wash your hands before handling food. Carry a small

Unclean hands are a leading source of illness on backpacking trips, so make sure you wash them well before handling food.

container of liquid soap (this tends to be a little easier to manage in the backcountry. Hard soap gathers dirt and pine needles and gets yucky without a soap container, which just adds weight to your pack). Wash your hands 200 yards from water sources to avoid contamination. Scrub for fifteen seconds or more to ensure you've cleaned them thoroughly, and make sure you've cleaned your nails as well.

Chapter Eight
Fires

Campfires are part of our camping traditions. People love to gather around the glow of the flames late into the evening sharing stories and the coziness the warmth creates. Fires are also destructive. Neglected campfires are one of the leading causes of wildfires in the United States, and campfires can leave behind unsightly scars and impacts in popular wilderness areas. You've seen them: trash-filled fire rings located right next to the edge of a lake or stream and blackened rock overhangs along the base of cliffs. The impacts are ugly and unnecessary. With a little knowledge and skill, you can enjoy a fire without causing lasting scars.

Fires can provide warmth and a cheery place to gather in the backcountry.

WHEN IS A CAMPFIRE APPROPRIATE?

Campfires are really only appropriate in places that have an adequate wood supply and where they are permitted by the managing agency. In the first case you'll have to use your judgment; in the second the rules are pretty clear. When the sign at the trailhead says No Fires, it means no fires. You'll get a ticket if you are found with a campfire in these areas unless it's an emergency.

There's no need to chop down trees or strip off branches to provide wood for a fire. If that's your only option, fires are not appropriate.

How much wood is adequate? If you see dead sticks lying around in abundance, there's enough wood. If you have to search for a long time to find some sticks or are tempted to strip dead limbs of standing trees, there's not enough wood around to support a fire.

SAFETY CONSIDERATIONS

Think before you start your fire. What's the weather doing? Is it windy? Is the forest dry from hot dry weather or years of drought? Are there a lot of dead trees from beetle kill? Is there a chance your fire could get out of control? If you have answered yes to these questions, you should probably reevaluate the safety of building a fire. Your best bet is to save your campfire for calm, cool nights in places where the forests are moist and the ground damp.

If you decide you are safe, make sure you have a container of water nearby to use in case the fire gets out of control.

LOW-IMPACT FIRES

The best place to build a fire is in a preexisting fire ring. Here the impacts have already occurred, so your fire will not add to the problem.

If you cannot find a fire pit and are still interested in a fire, you can make a platform from mineral soil

(dirt that contains little or no organic material) to hold your fire. Mound fires like these are easy to dismantle when you are done and leave no trace of your passing. Fire pans are also useful if you plan on building lots of fires. Mini backyard barbecue grills, aluminum roast-

ing pans, or metal oil-drain pans make good fire pans. You can punch holes in the corners of the pan and use string to attach it to your backpack. Fire pans should be lined with mineral soil or propped up on small rocks to avoid scorching the ground underneath.

COOKING ON FIRES

Cooking on fires can be fun, although dirty. You'll probably want to pack a stuff sack to carry your blackened pots in to avoid turning everything in your backpack black. Some people carry a lightweight grill to use over a fire, but unless you plan to cook on fires most of the time, that's an extravagance you can live without.

In lieu of a grill, you have two options. You can create a pseudo grill by making a tripod for your pot from three equal-sized rocks. Make sure the rocks are stable, so the pan doesn't tip over when you sneeze or make a minor adjustment to the setup. This method keeps your pot up above the heat source and allows you to replenish the fire as you cook if it becomes necessary. You can also create a bed of coals and place your pot directly on the hot coals. The only disadvantage to this technique is that you can't add more heat without removing your pot. I find the direct-coal method best suited for baking, when I want a low, steady heat source. Boiling water this way seems to take forever.

Use rocks to get your pot up above the fire.

Mound Fire How-To

Step 1: Gather a stuff sack full of mineral soil. What is mineral soil? It's dirt that contains little or no organic material. You can find mineral soil under the roots of fallen trees and on beaches, sandbars, and dry washes.

Step 2: Place a tarp or ground cloth over the surface where you plan to build your fire. Good fire sites include large rock slabs or non-vegetated dirt. Build a mound from your mineral soil approximately 2 feet across and 6 to 8 inches thick (you may need to make several trips to gather enough soil for your mound). You may also want to tuck the tarp under the soil to prevent rogue coals from burning a hole in it.

Step 3: Build your fire using small-diameter wood (in general, only use wood you can break easily with your hands—about wrist size in diameter). Make sure you gather dead and downed wood from a number of different locations to avoid depleting one area. Rotting wood provides vital nutrients to the soil so leave some behind.

Step 4: Enjoy your fire.

Step 5: Cleanup starts with burning all your wood down to ash. Scatter any unburned wood you may have gathered to help camouflage the site. Your ashes should be cool to the touch before you dispose of them. If they are still warm, douse them with water. Scatter the ashes far and wide, again to hide evidence of your fire. Gather up your mineral soil in the tarp and return it to its source. Camouflage the area by scattering duff and sticks and fluffing up trampled grass. Voilà! Your fireplace has disappeared.

Chapter Nine

Water Purification

Regardless of how clear and sparkly the water in the mountains may be, there's a chance it will make you sick if you drink it untreated. In the United States some bodies of water are contaminated by pathogens such as *giardiasis* or *cryptosporidiosis.* Unfortunately, you can't tell which ones without special tests, so most people recommend treating water in the wilderness.

BOILING

Water that reaches a rolling boil is safe to drink. You don't have to boil for any length of time or worry about altitude affecting temperature, the time and heat required to reach a boil is adequate to kill the things that will make you sick. Likewise, the process of cooking kills pathogens, so you don't need treated water to make pancake batter or dough.

CHEMICAL TREATMENT

There are a variety of chemical water-purification treatments available on the market, such as iodine tablets and chlorine drops. These treatments all work to kill most pathogens, although there are exceptions, so be sure to read the label thoroughly.

FILTERS

Filtering water is a great way to quench your thirst immediately. You just stick the filter in the stream, pump water into your bottle, and drink. The downsides are that filters are heavy and they tend to clog.

STERI-PENS

The newest, hottest water-treatment method on the market is the steri-pen, which uses ultraviolet light to kill pathogens. Steri-pens come in a portable size, and it takes less than a minute to purify your water. And like a filter, the steri-pen does not add any flavor to your drink. The downside is that you need to carry enough batteries to power the pen, and they do not work in cloudy, murky water.

Chapter Ten

Food Storage

Many animals have discovered that backpackers are an easy source of food. In the Rockies it's all too common to pull into camp, set down your backpack, and be greeted by a flock of gray jays searching for crumbs. Marmots chew holes in people's salty clothes in the Tetons, and mice crowd into shelters along the Appalachian Trail. These animals are really just pests and don't pose a great threat to your well-being, but they can be annoying and may destroy your gear or render your food inedible.

Bears are a different matter. Bears are dangerous when they come to associate humans with food, so having a bear raid your camp and make off with your meal is more than simply a nuisance. Both you and the bear can be in very real danger as a result of the encounter.

It's important, therefore, to pack your food so animals cannot get into it.

RODENT-PROOF FOOD STORAGE

Keeping rodents and birds (especially ravens) out of your food is tricky. These animals are experts at finding ways into food bags, and they can be quite difficult to combat if you camp at popular sites. The first step is to keep a clean kitchen and minimize odors that attract food robbers, but if the animals are habituated, that won't be enough. You may want to pack your food in some kind of plastic food-storage containers to keep the raiders at bay. Obviously, Rubbermaid and Tupperware containers are not the lightest or most convenient way to pack your food if you are trying to minimize weight, but in heavily used areas where animals have become problems, this is probably the best way to keep your food secure. You can also use bear canisters to protect your food against rodents and birds.

BEAR-PROOF STORAGE

In areas with bears public land managers typically mandate specific food-storage protocols. Many national parks now require all backpackers to carry specially designed bear canisters. In Yosemite National Park, the use of these canisters has been linked to an 85 percent decrease in the number of bear incidences, so it is worth the effort to use them. You can often rent bear canisters from the park service or from outfitters in the gateway communities. Check on the Internet before you go to figure out your options. However, if you expect to spend a lot of time camping in bear country, it is worth investing in your own canister.

People also hang food to secure it from bears, but in some places this technique is not that effective, particularly places like Yosemite, where the black bears have become experts at raiding food hangs. Grizzlies are not quite as adept at climbing, but you still need to have your food at least 15 feet off the ground and 7 feet from tree trunks or large branches. Effective bear hangs take practice and some technical expertise. For this reason bear canisters are highly recommended.

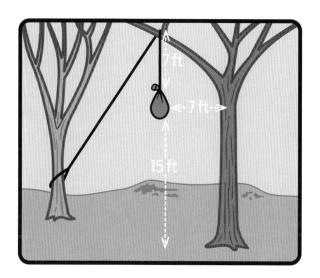

Cook and store your food at least 100 feet from your sleeping area. Even properly stored food may attract a curious bear, and you don't want to wake to find it sniffing around your tent as well.

Index

A

alcohol-burning stoves, 17, 18
aluminum cans and stoves, 17
aluminum roasting pans, 80

B

backpacks and gear, 10–13
Banks Fry/Bake pans, 40–41
bear canisters, 87, 88
bears, 8, 73, 87, 88–89
blended-fuel cartridge stoves, 17–19, 20, 23
bowls, 15
breads, 64
bulk foods and rationing, 24, 38–40, 42–47
burns, 37

C

calories, 30–31, 34, 65
campsites, 8–9
candy, 71
canister stoves, 18, 19
carbohydrates, 31
cheeses and meats, 68–69
chlorine drops, 84
cleanup
     dishes, 72–75
     fires, 83
     personal hygiene, 75–76
coals, 59, 62, 81
cookies, 71

cooking. *See also* recipes and cooking hints
     advanced, 38–56
     backcountry gourmet, 57–64
     baking, 41, 48–64, 81
     batter and dough consistencies, 60–61
     casseroles, 55–56
     frying, 47–48
     light and fast, 10–37
     portion sizes, 30
     techniques and tips, 33–34, 47–56, 60–61
cooking surfaces, durable, 7–9
crackers and breads, 68
cryptosporidiosis, 84
cups, 15, 16

D

dehydrated meals and sauce packets, 13, 24–25
dietary restrictions, 2, 4, 42
dishes, washing, 72–75

E

eating utensils, 15–17
energy bars, shots and gels, 69–70

F

fats in food, 31, 34
fire pans, 80
fire rings, 79

fires
    and ashes, 83
    campfires, 37, 77–83
    and cooking, 81
    low-impact, 79–80
    mound fires, 80,
        82–83
    twiggy fires, 59–64
    wildfires, 77
    and wood, 79, 83
food hangs, 88–89
food storage, 29–31, 86–89
fruit, dried, 68
frying pans and lids, 38,
    40–41, 47–54, 57–64
fuel conservation, 22

G
giardiasis, 84
gloves, wool, 41
goals, 2–3
gorp. *See* trail mixes
grills, 80, 81

I
international travel, 18, 23
iodine tablets, 84

K
kerosene, 18
kitchen lists, minimalist, 15
kitchen sites, choosing and
    organizing, 6–9
knives, 17

L
land management
    agencies, 8, 73, 78, 87
Leave No Trace principles,
    6–7

leftovers and food scraps,
    72, 73
lunches, 65–71

M
maintenance and repair
    kits for stoves, 23
meal planning, 24–32
menus, sample, 26–28
metal oil-drain pans, 80
mineral soil, 79–80, 82, 83
MSR WhisperLite, 20
multifuel-burning stoves,
    17, 18, 23
multitools, 17

N
Nalgene bottles, 45
National Outdoor
    Leadership School, 40
national parks, 87
nutritional concerns,
    31–32

O
Optimus 111B stoves, 14–16
Outback Oven, 58

P
packaging and repackaging
    food, 29, 45–47
pasta, 33, 36
pathogens, 84, 85
personal hygiene, 75–76
pie plates, 15
planning
    basic questions, 1–2,
        3–4
    food amounts, 30,
        43–45

meals, 24–32
preplanning for
bulk-rationing and
food, 42–45
plastic food-storage
containers, 87
plastic storage bags, 29,
45–47
pliers, 15
pot parkas, 57–59
pots and pans, 15, 22, 34,
37, 74–75
proteins, 31–32

Q
questionnaires, 2, 4, 26

R
recipes and cooking hints
Bean and Cornbread
Pie, 63
Calzones, 53
Cinnamon Rolls, 54
Lasagna, 55
Macaroni and Cheese,
36
Pizza, 52–53
rodents and birds, 86–87
Rubbermaid, 87

S
safety issues, 37, 79
snack mixes, 65–67
soap, 74, 76
solid-fuel-burning stoves
and tabs, 21
spices and spice kits, 34,
45, 46

spoons and spatulas, 15,
16–17
steri-pens, 86
stoves and fuel, 14–16,
17–23
stuff sack, 81, 82
sweet treats, 71

T
tarps and ground cloths,
82, 83
trail mixes, 67, 71
Tupperware, 87

U
U.S. Recommended Daily
Nutritional Allowances,
31

W
waste water disposal,
72–73
water bottles and
containers, 15, 16, 17
water contamination, 8
water filters, 85
water purification, 15, 34,
84–85
white-gas-burning stoves,
17, 20, 21, 23, 33, 48
windscreens, 22, 48, 49, 59
wood-burning stoves,
20–21

Y
Yosemite National Park,
87, 88